What is called
a kitchen
-- but really
is'nt
a kitchen
?

What is the
noisiest family
in the
world
?

What is a
battery
that makes music
?

Who could use
four pairs of hands
?
You'll find out
when you read...........→

LISL WEIL

Things that go Bang

McGRAW-HILL BOOK COMPANY
New York • Toronto • London • Sydney

Library of Congress Catalog Card Number: 76-80975

1234567890 HDEC 754321069

All kinds of things go bang!

Like doors . . .

or dishes. . . .

That's when Mother calls, "Stop that noise!
It's giving me a headache!"
Those are angry noises.
But there are other kinds of BANGS—
the kind people love to hear.

These are very special BANGS; they make fine music.
They have a rhythm and a sound all their own.
Musical BANGS are not just noise.
They may come marching in twos and threes, going,
"A-bang, a-bang, a-BOOM, BOOM, BOOM."
Or they may explode in a silvery clashy "TCHHINNN."
Or they may come rumbling out like faraway rolls of thunder.
But no matter how they sound,
musical BANGS are always exciting.
They color and accent the music,
just like a splash of bright color in a painting.

If you can learn to make musical BANGS,
you may become famous.
You will travel with lots of trunks and suitcases.
People will know you wherever you go.

Of course, it takes all kinds of musical instruments to make
musical BANGS.
Everyone has heard the big bass drum
or the bongo drum
or the tom-tom.
But there are many other instruments that make musical BANGS.
They are all part of one family—
the great family of PERCUSSION instruments.
And what is the meaning of *PERCUSSION?*
Why, it means "things that go BANG."

And once you know all about them ...

10

you may swing with a combo that plays jazz or rock music ...
or you may lead the parade in a marching band ...

. . . or you may be a PERCUSSIONIST
in a big orchestra, playing together
with a hundred other musicians.

You will be able to read notes—
the magic black and white dots
that spell out rhythm and melody
just as the letters of the alphabet
spell out the words of a story.

We hear a BANG when one thing strikes against another.
There are many different kinds of BANGS,

depending on what is being thumped (hands)

struck (sticks)

shushed (wire brushes)

tinkled (steel beater)

or boomed (foot pedal).

Some people think it is easy. It isn't.

A violinist plays only his fiddle, a bass player his double bass.
The clarinet player has only her clarinet.
But the PERCUSSIONIST must know how to play many
instruments. What's more, he must take them everywhere
he goes
to perform.

That is why he must travel
with so many suitcases and trunks.

Inside those trunks, the PERCUSSIONIST keeps a set of timpani (or kettle drums) — *and* a big bass drum,

and a triangle,
a tambourine,
and castanets ...

and a snare drum,

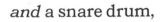

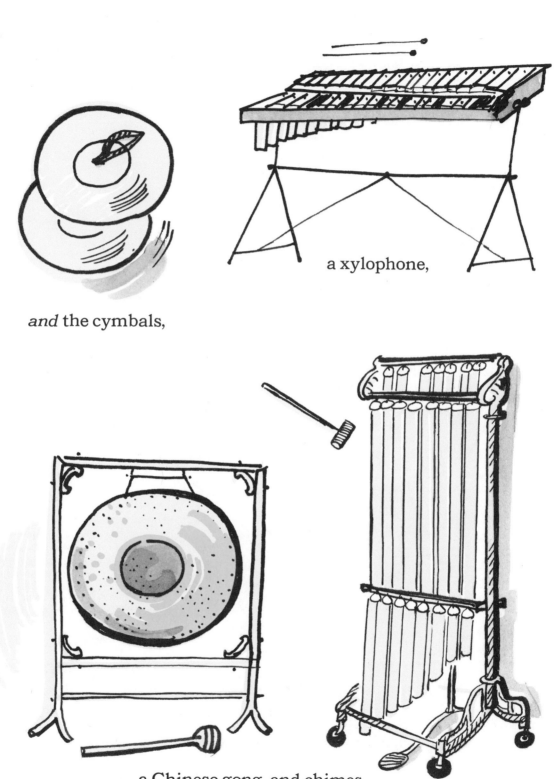

and the cymbals,

a xylophone,

a Chinese gong, and chimes.

The big kettle drums—called the timpani—look like soup kettles covered by sheets of thin plastic. Each kettle drum booms out a single deep tone. If the PERCUSSIONIST wants to make that tone higher or lower, he can tighten or loosen the screws that hold down the cover. There is also a foot pedal to help make the changes.

The PERCUSSIONIST in an orchestra may have to change the tone right in the middle of the music. That is why you often see him bending down to his kettle drum while everyone else is playing. He looks as if he were telling it a secret, but he is really trying out a new tone.

To play the kettle drum, the PERCUSSIONIST needs only his two drumsticks. But he can make many kinds of sounds with them. Using a drumstick tipped with hard felt, he can pound out a loud, heavy BANG. Using a drumstick tipped with soft lambswool, he can tap out a soft, dull bang. What with all the talk of kettles, bangs, clangs, and clatters, no wonder the PERCUSSION section is often called "the kitchen."

Other people call it "the battery,"
and with good reason.

The big bass drum can fill the air with the
mighty BOOMS of a battery, like the roar of
cannons.

The small snare drum goes RAT-TAT-TAT.
When you strike it, the strings on its side rattle
along. It makes you think of parades and of
keeping in step.

And don't forget:

The castanets—
wooden clappers that click
to the beat of the music.

The tambourine—
a small hoop covered
on one side with sheepskin.
When you slap it,
little metal plates
set into the hoop
jingle and rattle along.

The cymbals—
big metal plates that clang
and crash together.
What sharp, loud noises they make!

These are only some of the instruments the PERCUSSIONIST must know. Of course, no one expects him to play them all at the same time. He'd need many pairs of hands for that. Big orchestras sometimes have as many as three PERCUSSIONISTS performing at once.

The steel triangle goes ting-a-ling
when struck
by its steel beater.

While the Chinese gong
gives out a deep
and mysterious *BONNNGGG*.

The chimes are metal pipes
of different sizes.
When struck with a hammer,
each pipe sings out a different
tone that can make you think of
Christmas or of steeple bells.

You can play a merry tune
on the black and white bars
of the xylophone.

But whether working alone or in a group, the
PERCUSSIONIST is always busy. Even
when he seems to be resting, he is really
reading the music, watching the conductor,
waiting for the spot at which the timpani
must sound, or the cymbals clash.

25

Congolese drums

AFRICAN
RATTLES
AND BELLS

All of today's PERCUSSION instruments share a great
heritage from many lands and many cultures. Among the
proudest bearers of that heritage are the master drummers
of Africa.

26

TRIBAL DRUMS OF THE KINGDOM OF BURUNDI

GANKOGUI
double gong

THE SHAWARO
artistically decorated tin-
rattle, may be played
singly or in pairs.

THE agbe NIGERIAN
GOURD RATTLE

XYLOPHONE
from the SOUTH EAST COAST
OF AFRICA

These are PERCUSSIONISTS who can make their
drums sing, roar, whisper, or even tell a story.

Chinese Gong

EARLY WORSHIP

Kettle drums
brought Back from Arabia
By the Crusaders

Revolutionary
drum

Since the dawn of history, man has lived his life to the beat
of PERCUSSION. In every age, the strong rhythm of the
drum and the clash of cymbals have sent out calls to
worship or to war, to happiness or to sadness.
The ancient PERCUSSIONISTS used almost anything

INDIAN CEREMONIAL DRUM

Dancing to Castanets in Spain

Tyrolian Shoe-plattler

Conga drum

that went BANG. So does a modern PERCUSSIONIST. Quite a few of his instruments may even look like your little sister's toys—there may be rattles, wooden blocks, or sleigh bells. Anything can be used if it helps set the beat the music needs, the beat that people will follow.

What's that pounding in the next room? It's only another PERCUSSION instrument—the piano. Little sister wants to be a PERCUSSIONIST too. Every time she strikes a piano key, that key sets a thin hammer into action. The hammer strikes a metal string in turn, and little sister hears *another* wrong note. Don't worry. Practicing will help.

This instrument may look like a toy piano, but it's really a celesta. When you hit the keys, little hammers strike steel plates that tinkle out a sweet tune. The name *celesta* comes from an old word meaning "heavenly."

Even a typewriter can be a PERCUSSION instrument when played in rhythm with an orchestra. The rhythms are typed out; it's lots of fun to play *and* to listen to.

PERCUSSION helps composers paint pictures of happenings in history. *The 1812 Overture,* written by the composer Peter Tchaikovsky, tells us the story of a great war. There are no words. But in the beating of the drums, the clash of cymbals, and the ringing chimes, you can hear the roar of cannons, the clash of arms, and the cathedral bells mingling in a song of victory.

Listen to the pounding rhythms of a spring festival of long ago. They present a magic picture of the past.

The music was written by a composer of our own day, Igor Stravinsky. He wrote it for a ballet called *The Rite of Spring*.

Listen to all sorts of toys perform in *The Toy Symphony*, written by Leopold Mozart. Perhaps he was thinking of his own son, who grew up to be a great composer.

Are you ready to be a PERCUSSIONIST? If you are, you can make your own instruments. Then get some friends together and start your own kitchen combo.

Instruments:

1 strong table top
(hold also instruments)

2 frying pans
(to be struck back to back)

1 pot turned upside down on table (strike with spoon)

2 spoons any size --
must be good for striking tables, pots and water glasses.

1 pot or saucepan (covered) filled with noisemakers = use buttons or dried beans (jerk sharply up and down)

1 covered cookie tin with 12 coins, buttons, or dried beans inside (tap with spoon or shake hard)

4 water glasses of same size
 1 empty
 1 two-thirds full of water
 1 three-quarters full of water
 1 completely full of water
(tap very gently with spoon)

Gather your instruments on a table. Divide your group into
BAKERS and **COOKS**, and try out the *March for Kitchen* Combo on page 37.

Remember: all good Percussionists practice with the door shut.

The BAKERS take the top line, the COOKS take the lower
line. Then both teams switch over. If you're playing
alone, try first the top, then the bottom line.

How to play:

First, choose your instrument and find its matching sign below:

table top

pot, upside-down on table

frying pans

waterglasses

covered saucepan, filled with beans, etc.

cookie tin

spoons

Look at the MARCH FOR KITCHEN COMBO on the opposite page. Do you see the numbers that count out 1-2, 1-2? These set the *beat* of the music. Start in by counting 1-2, 1-2 steadily and you'll have the beginnings of a fine march.

Each count of 1-2 makes up a *measure*. To find out when to play within the measure, follow the signs as you count. Your team may play on the first beat only, on both beats, or not at all. If you're playing the glasses, pot, or table top, watch the spoon signs. One spoon ♪ means "strike once per count." Two spoons ♪♪ mean "strike twice per count." The *rest* sign ⌇ means "take a rest." when you see this sign, do not play anything at all.

Example:

means: First the COOKS beat the frying pans together *once* on the count of 1 while the BAKERS rest.

　　Then the BAKERS strike the pot *once* on the count of 2 while the COOKS rest.

means: The BAKERS strike the pot *twice* on the count of 1 and *twice* again on the count of 2.

　　The COOKS beat the frying pans together *once* on the count of 1 and *once* on the count of 2.

36

MARCH FOR KITCHEN COMBO
by David Shapiro

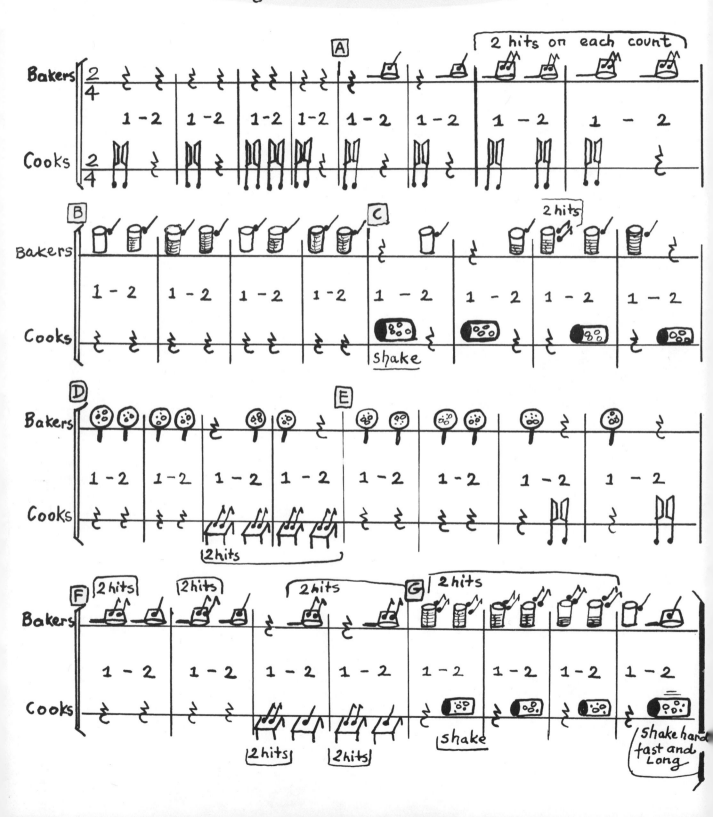

So you see, BANGS can be wonderful sounds
if you know how to make them the right way.
But as long as you're learning, just remember:
A good PERCUSSIONIST always practices behind closed doors.

THE PERCUSSIONIST'S GUIDE TO PRONUNCIATION

timpani—TIM-puh-nee

bass drum—BAYSS drum

snare drum—SNAYR drum

triangle—TRY-an-gul

tambourine—tam-buh-REEN

castanets—kass-tuh-NETS

cymbals—SIM-buls

xylophone—ZY-loh-fohn

Chinese gong—CHY-nees GAHNG

piano—PYAN-oh

celesta—che-LESS-tuh

chimes—CHY-ms

agbe—ah-gbeh

gankogui—gahn-KOH-gwee

shawaro—sha-woh-ROH

See next page

The Percussion Family